Poetic Pearls & Gems With Purpose

POETIC PEARLS & GEMS WITH PURPOSE

Pearly Gates Publishing LLC, Houston, Texas

Poetic Pearls & Gems With Purpose

Copyright © 2016
Angela R. Edwards

All Rights Reserved.
No portion of this publication may be reproduced, stored in any electronic system, or transmitted in any form or by any means (electronic, mechanical, photocopy, recording, or otherwise) without written permission from the publisher. Brief quotations may be used in literary reviews.

ISBN 10: 1945117397
ISBN 13: 9781945117398
Library of Congress Control Number: 2016950241

For information and bulk ordering, contact:
Pearly Gates Publishing LLC
Angela R. Edwards, CEO
P.O. Box 62287
Houston, TX 77205
BestSeller@PearlyGatesPublishing.com

Poetic Pearls & Gems With Purpose

DEDICATION

Poetic Pearls & Gems With Purpose
is dedicated to the **Poet, Lyricist**, and
Versifier in everyone.
Due to the freedoms of prose associated
with poetry, may you, too, realize the
power of the written word.

Poetic Pearls & Gems With Purpose

ACKNOWLEDGEMENTS

First, giving **ALL** honor, glory, and praise to our Heavenly Father. Without God, we *are* nothing. Without God, we can *do* nothing. Appreciation and love, Lord, for sound minds and abilities to share with and encourage others.

I wish to extend a **HUGE** *THANK YOU* to each of the Co-Authors who made significant contributions to this project. Without hesitation, each of them presented written works that are sure to connect with others.

To Arieon Burns: You are the youngest contributor to this project and provided very mature poetry for the readers.

To Arlene Holden: I truly appreciate your continued support and ensuring the family legacy is forever imprinted in black and white.

Poetic Pearls & Gems With Purpose

To James Mitchell: Your wisdom and pizzazz with the written word is amazing!

To Johnson Jones: The strength of your personal spiritual walk is evident in your poetry. Your words of encouragement are appreciated.

To Juanita Flores: You could not have written about a timelier and necessary topic: Love.

To Keri Myuda: Writing from each end of the spectrum (love and hate) is sure to connect with the masses.

To Loyce Bullock: The variety of topics you presented will surely enhance the lives of many.

To Marlowe Scott: Your God-inspired and original poetry is reflective of your loving heart for your fellow man and fellow woman.

Poetic Pearls & Gems With Purpose

To Steven Jackson: Your work speaks to the heart of "man" and will surely bless others as they do their own self-reflection.

Poetic Pearls & Gems With Purpose

INTRODUCTION

"Publishing a volume of verse is like dropping a rose petal down the Grand Canyon and waiting for the echo."
~ Don Marquis ~

Poetry. Prose is the author's choosing. *Funny thing about poetry:* There is no right or wrong way for it to be presented.

Thoughts flow freely. They are inspired by moments in time, waiting with anticipation for the poet to pen the words that will free the minds of others.

Some poems are written from experience. Others are penned by dreamers. Still others are simply a longing for the betterment of critical aspects of our lives.

Each type is presented in *Poetic Pearls & Gems With Purpose.*

Poetic Pearls & Gems With Purpose

Dear Reader, you are encouraged to look deep within your own soul as you delve into the hearts and minds of the authors through the written word. Be ever-mindful there is **power** in words. Don't just aimlessly flip through each poem while thinking it doesn't apply to you. There is something for everyone - and that means **YOU**, too. Take the time to appreciate the efforts of those whose desires are to uplift and inspire you on life's journey.

- ➤ Make note of the different styles of writing.

- ➤ Pay special attention to the eloquent use of words.

- ➤ Feel the author's heartbeat with each syllable.

Poetic Pearls & Gems With Purpose

Then, when the process is complete, you are encouraged to write what **YOU** *feel*. Share it with others. You never know what another needs unless you take a leap of faith and expose your heart for them to see!

Be blessed and be a blessing to others - through the **POWER OF YOUR WRITTEN WORD!**

"Poetry is everywhere; it just needs editing."
~ James Tate ~

Poetic Pearls & Gems With Purpose

TABLE OF CONTENTS

Dedication _____ vi

Acknowledgements _____ vii

Introduction _____ x

Table of Contents _____ 13

PURPOSE GEM: ENCOURAGEMENT _____ 1

WE BOUNCE BACK _____ 2

WELL DONE _____ 4

SONGS IN THE NIGHT _____ 6

THE WEIGHT OF HATE _____ 9

YOU DECIDED TO MOVE ON _____ 11

LIVE, RIDE, AND DIE _____ 13

PURPOSE GEM: FAMILY LOVE _____ 15

MY SPECIAL COUSIN _____ 16

MY ONLY SON... _____ 18

GOD'S CHILD _____ 18

MY CHILD...GOD'S CHILD _____ 20

FLOWERS FOR MOM _____ 22

ANGEL IN YOUR MIDST _____ 25

BECAUSE YOU'RE MY KIN _____ 27

PURPOSE GEM: FRIENDSHIP _____ 29

Poetic Pearls & Gems With Purpose

WE'RE AWFULLY GLAD YOU PASSED OUR WAY	30
FOR LETTING ME SERVE YOU	32
PURPOSE GEM: HEALING	33
SO FAR AWAY THAT YOU CAN'T HEAR	34
INSIDE I CRY	36
ABUSE IS NOT LOVE	38
THOSE ARE YOUR FEET THAT I FEEL	40
STILL I AWAKE	41
PURPOSE GEM: IN MEMORIAM	43
MY TRIBUTE TO MOTHER ETHEL B. JONES	44
REMEMBERING DADDY'S DAY	45
PURPOSE GEM: LOVE & LIFE	47
I FEEL YOU	48
AS I LAY	50
ADULTHOOD REALITY	52
LOVE IS WHAT IT IS	54
PURPOSE GEM: SALVATION & SPIRITUALITY	55
CALVARY'S CROSS	56
THANK YOU FOR HIM	58
THE SHEEPFOLD	59
MORE THAN YOU KNOW	61
JESUS, MY FRIEND JESUS	63

Poetic Pearls & Gems With Purpose

HIGHER SPIRITUAL HEIGHTS	*65*
GROWING IN FAITH	*67*
PURPOSE GEM: SPECIAL ADDITIONS	*69*
SAVE THE CHILDREN, STOP THE VIOLENCE,	
KEEP THE PEACE	*70*
THE DEVIL GOES TO CHURCH	*73*
CONCLUSION	*83*
PURPOSE GEM: PEN YOUR POEM	*85*
APPENDIX	*93*
ABOUT THE COMPILER	*94*
CONNECT WITH PEARLY GATES PUBLISHING LLC	*96*

Poetic Pearls & Gems With Purpose

PURPOSE GEM:

ENCOURAGEMENT

Poetic Pearls & Gems With Purpose

WE BOUNCE BACK

JOHNSON JONES © 2016

When in doubt and it looks as if
there's no way out,
I look to God - the One I
cannot do without.
My Lord. My Savior. My Redeemer.
The One who gave wisdom to
Joseph the Dreamer.

They may laugh. They may scoff.
They may even betray;
But my Lord is always there - leading me
every step of the way.
Higher and higher, we bounce back.
After all that we go through,
we never truly lack.

What's for me is for me.
What's for you is for you.
No devil in Hell has the authority to stop
our breakthroughs.
Higher and higher, we bounce back;
Keeping our eyes on the prize…no
backtrack.

Purpose Gem: Encouragement

Eternal life with our Father in Heaven;
That's **my** heart's desire.
My spirit is ***LIT***! My spirit is ***HOT***!
My spirit is on ***FIRE***!

Higher and higher, we bounce back.
My Lord. My Friend. My Father.
The **ONE** who covers us **ALL**
when we are under attack.

Poetic Pearls & Gems With Purpose

WELL DONE
LOYCE BULLOCK © 2016

Right from the start, you began to climb
The ladder to glory, step by step;
You headed for the finish line
Looking to God, being sure
you were kept.

Satan unleashed his royal counterfeit,
And down the ladder you came
Being hesitant to wait,
to set us all straight.
You immediately took on a new name.

In reality, things around you
were going different.
Through your eyes, you saw
them the same.
The order to search and seek
set before you;
Into your mind, the thought
never came.

Purpose Gem: Encouragement

Now, looking straight up
to the top of the ladder,
You see the place that you fell from.
There's a need to repent
and your will to relent
To hear God again say, *"Well Done!"*

Poetic Pearls & Gems With Purpose

SONGS IN THE NIGHT

Marlowe R. Scott © 2016

God speaks to me in many pleasant ways
Throughout each day and night;
Through the whispering trees and
flowering fields,
Babbling brooks and lovely, chirping
birds in flight.

Often in the quiet stillness of the night,
My Heavenly Father
also speaks from above
With *beautiful* words, melodies, and songs
That inspire and confirm
His unending love.

Songs that my mother once sang
Or those I learned as a child;
All of those precious renderings
Have comforted me through many a trial.

Purpose Gem: Encouragement

The drums, tambourine, flute, and pipe;
The harp, timbrel, trumpet, and lyre -
Many musical instruments
are in God's Holy Word,
All making a joyful noise
to set my soul on fire!

The Bible's Old Testament
as well as the New
Tell of melodies and songs of praise,
as well as blessings,
That many such as Moses, Isaiah,
and David offered
For strength and protection from
Lucifer's *attempted* messings.

Even one of troubled Job's
young friends, Elihu,
Acknowledged that God giveth songs in
the night (Job 35:10);
In the end, Job's blessings increased two-
fold (Job 42:10);
*Who wouldn't trust and serve a God with
that power and might?*

Poetic Pearls & Gems With Purpose

So just listen, my sisters and brothers,
As God speaks to you in
His various ways;
Remember: His messages are clear,
tried, and true;
Seek to hear, oh hear Him,
each and every day.

Purpose Gem: Encouragement

THE WEIGHT OF HATE
KERI MYUDA © 2016

There's so much *hatred*
in the world today.
My heart is pained at the very thought of
how things have gone awry…again.
People quote the Constitution
as their legal "right to hate"
And spew out hurtful words -
and actions to follow - that pain
both women and men.

Our children are lost and confused.
They are being taught to hate
when their nature is to love.
Our Heavenly Father **MUST** be crying
As He looks down on the
world from above.

What can we do? What can we say?
How are we to live our lives this way?
The love I feel for my fellow man is
feeling useless,
As we go about looking over our
shoulders at those who are ruthless.

Poetic Pearls & Gems With Purpose

Ruthless with their words. Ruthless with their thoughts.
Without a care in the world, they tear down others.
Ruthless with their words. Ruthless with their thoughts.
Without a care in the world, they harm our sisters and brothers.

Let's learn to love again and spread messages of *hope*.
Let's learn to love again and share God's *Good News*!
Let's learn to love again and rid the world of **hate**
So that our youth can know love unconditional - and love others without *the weight of hate*.

Purpose Gem: Encouragement

YOU DECIDED TO MOVE ON
LOYCE BULLOCK © 1998

There are things that pushed you each
and every day,
And it really didn't matter when things
got in your way.
You held your head up strong and proud,
and focused your weary eyes
On the goals set in front of you, no matter
what the size.

You worked and toiled long and hard to
accomplish all those goals.
The desires just kept on growing; they
never ever grew old.
You stood right still in motion until the
door was opened wide.
As soon as the door was opened, you
eagerly stepped right inside.

Poetic Pearls & Gems With Purpose

We know it wasn't easy, but the experiences were great.
Encouragement never came your way - or it was sometimes too late.
Looking back over your shoulder at the road you left behind,
You wonder how you made it…without losing your mind.

You did not come this far in life without making a big wave.
You've sometimes swallowed all your pride, your dignity to save.
To look for you in this place again, we miss you; you are gone.
God gave you this wonderful choice…
You Decided to Move On.

Purpose Gem: Encouragement

LIVE, RIDE, AND DIE
JAMES MITCHELL © 2016

I live, I ride, and I am Christian.

I live, I ride, and I am American.

I live, I ride, and I am the future.

I live, I ride, and I am young, gifted, and Black.

I live, I ride, and I am mature, experienced, and ready.

I live, I ride, and I am diligent, unstoppable, and determined.

I live, I ride, and I am always willing and able to make the change.

I live, I ride, and I am all this because I am **God's** child until the day I die!

Poetic Pearls & Gems With Purpose

PURPOSE GEM:

FAMILY LOVE

Poetic Pearls & Gems With Purpose

MY SPECIAL COUSIN
ARLENE HOLDEN © 2004

I have a cousin named Marlowe Ray.
She is one in a million, is all that I say.
She is witty and pretty -
and that is not all:
She has awards and certificates, I recall.
She has achieved, achieved, achieved.

We are related by the Winrow line.
A personality such as
Marlowe's is hard to find.
She works very diligently with her hands,
And for her Lord at His commands.

A coward she is not;
if Marlowe has to do it,
She will give it all she's got.
She was born with talent, poise, and such;
My cousin, Marlowe, is just too much!

Purpose Gem: Family Love

Cedarville is her place of birth,
Which is one of the best towns
on God's green Earth.
Here she lived and went to school,
And was taught to practice the
"Golden Rule".

At that time she did not know
When she grew up where she would go.

God has blessed her
and protected her life;
She lives without envy, malice, and strife.

There are many good things that can be
said about Marlowe Ray,
But this is all I am going to say today.

Poetic Pearls & Gems With Purpose

MY ONLY SON... GOD'S CHILD
LOYCE BULLOCK © 2002

Would I be so bold to compare you to
Another blessed Son that I know,
Who bled and died upon
that old rugged cross -
His powerful love for us He did show?

Born only one step up from a manger,
No heat from the animal's nose.
Somehow it struck me as being the same
That the weather that day was very cold.

I remember the day so *distinctly*.
Its print is stamped forever in my heart.
How you made your way into
this cruel world that day
Without too much of a start.

I was truly alone that day you were born;
Silently I shed a bucket of tears.
It only took me a few minutes to know
This son would bless me, too,
through the years.

Purpose Gem: Family Love

It was a few new clothes and a lotta
hand-me-downs.
Your first shoes were not a lot to pay,
But I rejoiced in my heart right
from the start:
God had given **me** a son on that day!

So, when I question the Lord…
if He loves me,
He gives me some time
to myself to reflect
About another cold day in December -
Then all my thoughts of
self-pity I neglect.

As you grow to be a real man of God,
If you should wonder in this life
if you have won,
Call me up or just think of your Mother…
The day God gave me **YOU**,
My Blessed Son.

Poetic Pearls & Gems With Purpose

MY CHILD...GOD'S CHILD
LOYCE BULLOCK © 2002

The 5th of September was a beautiful day,
When into this world,
Shannon made her way.
I didn't know the Lord then,
so I thought only joy
Would come in my life
in the form of a boy.
But God's infinite wisdom,
blessed with a pearl
To enrich my whole life
in the form of a girl.

As my eyes looked upon you
for the very first time,
You were perfect and beautiful -
only one-of-a-kind.
There will never be a person
born in this world
Who can stand and measure up
to my little girl.

Purpose Gem: Family Love

There are so many things that
I admire about you;
If I shared it with thousands,
I would never be through.
Some can't see your perfection.
In their eyes, this is true;
But they don't have the same
love for you as I do.

From that very first day,
you had a mind of your own;
Only finding out at times you did
some things wrong.
But nevertheless, my love
for you stayed strong -
Encouraging your efforts
to stand up and go on.

All these years of your life, you have
graciously blessed
My heart as your mother…
through many a test.
The title of *"Little Girl"*,
28 years you have worn;
And I thank God above -
you are my first born.

Poetic Pearls & Gems With Purpose

FLOWERS FOR MOM
ANGELA EDWARDS © 2016

Flower: Baby's Breath
I'm not going to wait to give
flowers to my mother.
She was God's gift to ME - she's one-of-a-kind…unlike any other.
There's never been a moment
when she hasn't cared;
Her unconditional love - since before my
birth - has always been there.

Flower: Daisy
Was life always a breeze?
Did we always "get along"?
The answer to both is "no" -
but we remained strong!
No devil in Hell could destroy
that which GOD ordained:
With Mom Marlowe by my side,
we will strut unashamed.

Purpose Gem: Family Love

Flower: Lily

Blossoming and blooming,
reaching for the sky…
My days are filled with light -
and let me tell you why!
Mom Marlowe is so full of life and brings
joy to the hearts of many!
I have no doubt the memories of her from
others are just as legendary!

Flower: Rose

I'm all grown up now - a woman of God
walking a path all my own.
I was prepared for this journey by a
mother who has a strong backbone.
Mom Marlowe is faith-filled and shares
God's glory at every turn;
To live my life pleasing to God is my
heart's desire and greatest concern.

Poetic Pearls & Gems With Purpose

Flower: Tulip

As the sun rises and the suns sets,
I am forever glad
For GOD'S choice of a mother for ME -
through the good times and the bad.
I love you, Mom Marlowe; these flowers
have bloomed just for you.
Take a moment to appreciate the
fragrance of each one - and in doing so,
know that my love for you is true.

Purpose Gem: Family Love

ANGEL IN YOUR MIDST
LOYCE BULLOCK © 2002

My, My, My…Sweet, Little Guyler.
The years have gone so fast
It only seems like yesterday,
But 11 years have passed!

You are a blessed child in many ways.
Most people don't really know
The treasures inside you
came from above
Only through eyes of love they show.

The nasty burdens you are
forced to carry,
Most adults will say, "*Oh, boy!*"
But with the grace of God
surrounding you,
All that you feel is the joy.

As we share with you our hearts of love -
As parents and loved-ones should do -
We give our thanks to the Faithful One
For 11 years, His hands are on you.

Poetic Pearls & Gems With Purpose

When thoughts arise how you got here
Pushing through our lives like this,
The answer comes in a still, small voice,
"I placed an Angel in Your Midst."

Purpose Gem: Family Love

BECAUSE YOU'RE MY KIN
LOYCE BULLOCK © 2016

I looked up to you for such a long time.
I thought you much better than me,
So I long overlooked many
things have I took;
You believed that's the way
you should be.

I overlooked the way you
used your folks;
Tricked to think we were using you.
With your chest stuck out proud
And your head held real high,
Living too hard not to die.

As I quietly went along with the things
you did wrong,
Your life was really a mess.
As I opened my eyes,
I was truly surprised…
The correction held close to my chest.

Poetic Pearls & Gems With Purpose

Now I know what is right;
I can see what is wrong.
This lesson I have taken within,
For it grieves me to see
the blame is on me…
Letting you slide because you're my kin.

PURPOSE GEM:

FRIENDSHIP

Poetic Pearls & Gems With Purpose

WE'RE AWFULLY GLAD YOU PASSED OUR WAY

LOYCE BULLOCK © 1997

Sometimes in life, friends will appear;
Some from far and some from near.
They come together from the very start,
Never intending to share their hearts.

But as the days go slowly by,
Your feelings change and
you wonder why
You're very different, yet you're the same.
Not just in looks, but also in name.

Your thoughts on matters belong to you,
But before you know it,
you're sharing them, too.
It's a wonderful way for friends to bond;
In all that you do, you will become one.

Purpose Gem: Friendship

When friends are together,
it's always a test
And working with friends
brings out the best.
It teaches you how to be firm and strong.
It teaches when to push it
or leave it alone.

Whatever the occasion,
you're not just our friend.
We've become family,
and to that there's no end.
Though we'll miss you terribly
and wish you would stay,
We're awfully glad you passed our way.

Poetic Pearls & Gems With Purpose

FOR LETTING ME SERVE YOU

LOYCE BULLOCK © 2016

These small things in this basket
Do not come alone.
It shares a great big **THANK YOU**
Now that you're in your new home.

The Wine represents the blood of Christ.
The glasses for you makes
the drinking nice.
The gift card and popcorn to share a
moment together.
The candles to light your path in
inclement weather.
The fruit will always represent your
prosperity alone,
As God truly blesses you
in your new home.

PURPOSE GEM:

HEALING OF THE HEART, MIND, AND SPIRIT

Poetic Pearls & Gems With Purpose

SO FAR AWAY THAT YOU CAN'T HEAR

LOYCE BULLOCK © 2016

For many days I've called you;
My body…it grows weak.
My words to you continually,
Now I can hardly speak.

I humbly ask you to tell me:
What wrong have I done
While on this path I journey,
Along this race I run?

You continue to ignore me,
Though it's only you I seek.
I'm calling on your Holy Name;
You've not answered in a week.

Everything around me is slowly dying;
Prosperity is totally lost.
Was this really what you meant
When you said, *"Count out the cost"*?

Purpose Gem: Healing

Some of your children depend on me;
In turn, I'm believing you.
The promises that were made for me
To do what you asked me to do.

Why is it now you've turned your back?
You no longer want me near,
So is it me or is it you who is
So far away that you can't hear?

INSIDE I CRY
LOYCE BULLOCK © 2016

I looked upon your beautiful flesh,
Traces of sin in every place.
I feel inside the urge to tell you
About God's Amazing Grace.

You look so cold everywhere you go;
Inside your heart I can see a tear.
It's been so long since you've been warm,
It doesn't matter what time of year.

Your hands are worn, the calluses show,
The liaisons are running and ripe.
This did not come from
your working hard:
It came from hitting the pipe.

I see the pain upon your face.
You don't like what's holding you;
And looking back where you came from,
You're much better than what you do.

Purpose Gem: Healing

I want to reach out and take your hand
To say the way you are is a lie,
But I just drive on in my cute little car…
And down deep inside, I cry.

Poetic Pearls & Gems With Purpose

ABUSE IS NOT LOVE
MARLOWE R. SCOTT © 2015

Abuse comes in many forms.
In some cultures and homes,
Abuse is the norm.

It's directed at children and adults, too;
Has abuse ever happened to you?

Have scars - seen and unseen -
Impacted this earthly life?
Have loved-ones inflicted pains
causing deep strife?

What to do? Where to turn for relief?
Will anyone believe my deepening grief?

There has to be a way to make
it through another day.
Help me, Dear Lord: Help me, I pray.

I have heard about Jesus
And how He came to save us.

Purpose Gem: Healing

Is Jesus the answer for me?
If so, this is my plea:

Help me, Dear Jesus.
Help me right now.
At your throne I throw my cares
and humbly bow.

Please relieve the pain; make it go away.
I believe you can, and this I pray:

"Thank you for the warm comfort
I now feel.
Thank you, Dear Jesus,
because I know you can heal.
Take my abuser under your care,
So that no one else will
feel the pains I bear."

Poetic Pearls & Gems With Purpose

THOSE ARE YOUR FEET THAT I FEEL
LOYCE BULLOCK © 2016

From the time I can remember,
It's always been the same.
I was the one to think of it…
You put it in your name.

Choosing those things that suited me,
You proudly displayed they suited you;
From hair and clothes and bigger things,
It happens in all that I do.

That special thing God put in me;
He made me one-of-a-kind.
And every time you stole my thoughts,
I thought I was losing my mind.

Now that I've gotten older,
I have searched to know the deal.
I found the pain is not inside:
Those are your feet that I feel.

Purpose Gem: Healing

STILL I AWAKE
JOYCE BULLOCK © 2016

As I lay last night
In the image of death,
The weight of the world lay with me.
The confusion in time
Runs through my mind;
It doesn't take the eyes to see.

I finally give in to the pressure;
The darkness is beginning to engulf me.
So I lay there in style…
Semi-peace for a while -
For just a few minutes, I'm free.

I rejoice and give thanks
To my Maker and such;
For a time, I wallow in this place
To the peace that it brings
And for righteousness' sake,
It's morning and STILL, I awake.

Poetic Pearls & Gems With Purpose

PURPOSE GEM:

IN MEMORIAM

Poetic Pearls & Gems With Purpose

MY TRIBUTE TO MOTHER ETHEL B. JONES

MARLOWE R. SCOTT © 2016

Mother Ethel B. Jones
is rejoicing in Heaven
In that special place prepared just for her!
We were blessed to have had her with us
Before she went with Jesus up there.

She was Tabernacle Baptist Church's
First Lady
And our loving Church Mother, as well.
She was with us in joys and sorrows, too;
Ready for words of encouragement
And to ask each one, "*How are you?*"

We shall miss her presence among us,
But we find contentment in knowing
Our Beloved Mother Ethel B. Jones
Now has eternity's best…
As in the arms of our Savior,
She has found eternal rest!

Purpose Gem: In Memoriam

REMEMBERING DADDY'S DAY...

ANGELA EDWARDS © 2016

James W. Boyce was God's choice.
Father and friend until the end.

The day he suddenly passed away had
been filled with joy…
That was nothing unusual from that
"good, old boy"!
He was always smiling and full of cheer -
Not letting on the status of his health
was rather severe.

I can imagine him thinking,
"I don't want her to worry about me.
I'll keep my pain hush-hush.
I'm sure she would agree."

Having just spoken with him
just a few hours before,
When I received the call that he was gone,
I quickly crumbled to the floor.

Poetic Pearls & Gems With Purpose

What did she say?
My daddy had a **WHAT**?
A heart attack? No way! He was healthy -
yet I knew in my gut...
He was aging and truly had lived
his life to the fullest.
That didn't stop the news of his passing
pierce through me like a hail of bullets.

James W. Boyce is no longer here.
His spirit lives on in those
who held him close and dear.

The memories of Daddy live on
through fond recollections
Of days of old and happy reflections.
His love lives on through the three
generations he left behind.
Daddy, you're forever in my heart and
always on my mind.

PURPOSE GEM:

LOVE & LIFE

Poetic Pearls & Gems With Purpose

I FEEL YOU

JUANITA FLORES © 2016

When you cry, I feel you.

When you laugh, I hear you.

When you love, I feel you.

When you smile, I see you.

When you are far, I yearn for you.

When you are near, I notice you.

Emotions… As raw as freshly-picked fruit. I wear them on my sleeve.

You are the reason I rise in the morning. Not a day goes by that I do not remember the "whys" and the "hows" of you coming to be part of my life.

I thank God for you.

Purpose Gem: Love & Life

I thank God for your tears, laughter, love, smiles, distance, AND closeness.

Have I told you lately that I feel you?

In case you forgot all that
God ordained for US to BE:
I FEEL YOU.

Do YOU feel ME?

AS I LAY
ARIEON BURNS © 2016

As I lay breathing slowly,
Not wanting to breath at all,
I close my eyes, I see you -
Young, healthy, full of life.
I can only see clips of you,
But that's all I need…to keep breathing.

I smile as I watch you.
I can feel your faint touch
As you wrap your arms around me.
You tell me everything will be okay;
I believe you.

You lie, but for my own good.
Your warmth surrounds me.
I begin to fall into a deep sleep,
Wanting you to stay, not leave.
I quickly hug you back -
Not letting go.

Purpose Gem: Love & Life

Slipping into darkness…
Watching you fade away…
But knowing you will always be with me
As I lay.

Poetic Pearls & Gems With Purpose

ADULTHOOD REALITY

STEVEN JACKSON © 2016
SDJBOOKS.COM

Years passed like the rocks that erode.
Why, when you are young,
you wish to be old?
When you are old,
wished you were young.
Bright, vibrant like the sun.
Used to run freely all day, now you
cough up a lung.
Consequences enhance from
right and wrong.
No longer looked upon as the clumsy
one, though it did not fade
As decision after decision is made.
Does my age prevent my dreams
I am pursuing?
There is always more I could be doing.
Welcome to adulthood,
land of misery and bills…
And lack of time - mentally.
Wanting the opposite sex - physically.
Endeavor for marriage,
the great big mystery.

Purpose Gem: Love & Life

Life is a mystery, oh yes, it is.
Have a dream about it,
and (pause) wake up with a kid.
Work too hard, you want to
enjoy life as a kid.
(But you are) stuck in this revolving loop
wishing you could say you did.

Poetic Pearls & Gems With Purpose

LOVE IS WHAT IT IS

KERI MYUDA © 2016

Love is…*GOD*.
Love is…*JESUS*.
Love is…*THE HOLY SPIRIT*.
Love is freely given to us.

Love is…*FREE*.
Love is…*FOR ALL*.
Love is…*UPLIFTING*.
Love picks me up when I fall.

Love is…*SWEET*.
Love is…*KIND*.
Love is…*COMFORTING*.
Thoughts of love fill my mind.

Love is all that and more;
This one thing I know for sure…
It feels so good to be loved
And even better from our
Heavenly Father from up above.

PURPOSE GEM:

SALVATION & SPIRITUALITY

Poetic Pearls & Gems With Purpose

CALVARY'S CROSS

MARLOWE R. SCOTT © 2016

The song-writer wrote,
"There's a cross for everyone".
Yes, crosses for you and me;
The crosses we bear may be many,
But each has a message and lesson,
you see.

There is a cross that is more precious
than them all -
It is the Cross on Calvary.
That rugged cross that our Savior bore
To save sinners like you and me.

Jesus was crucified on that cross
On the hill named Calvary.
As between two sinners the cross stood
As He bore the sins for you and me.

Purpose Gem: Salvation & Spirituality

He died and was placed
in a borrowed tomb
Where His body stayed until
early on the third day.
Then, He rose with all authority in
Heaven and Earth
On that very first Easter Day!

After 40 days before
His ascension to Glory,
Jesus promised the Holy Spirit's
power would come
So that mankind would become
witnesses in all the Earth
Because of Salvation given
by God's One and Only Son.

Now, we must seek forgiveness
and tell the world
That the free gift of Salvation is here
To anyone admitting sin
and believing in Jesus -
The One who sacrificed His life because
He loved us so dear.

Poetic Pearls & Gems With Purpose

THANK YOU FOR HIM

JAMES MITCHELL © 2016

Thank you for Him.

Born in a manger to conceal Him;

Staged and stabbed on a cross

to reveal Him.

Miraculously dispatched as a Spirit so

that all can feel Him.

Painstakingly forgives a nation to be

forever relational to Him.

Soon and very soon, the eternally-blessed

will be destined to be with Him.

Behold, a virgin shall bring forth a son,

and they shall call Him 'Emanuel'.

Purpose Gem: Salvation & Spirituality

THE SHEEPFOLD
MARLOWE R. SCOTT © 2015

Being a part of the Lord's Sheepfold
Is a very blessed thing
Because our Redeemer, Jesus,
Is the Keeper, Savior, and King!

When we are lost, Jesus finds us.
He picks us up and carries us back.
With Him as Protector and Leader,
No good thing shall we lack.

He is tender, gentle, and kind.
He loves us and calls each by name.
Surely, Jesus knows the pastures we need
To maintain our naïve
and earthly frames.

We can sleep peacefully at night
Under the Shepherd's watchful eye.
The dawning of each new day
Guarantees that He is still nearby.

Poetic Pearls & Gems With Purpose

Do not be caught outside the Sheepfold;
There are dangers and death out there!
Come and stay safely inside with us
Until we transcend to Eternity in the air!

Purpose Gem: Salvation & Spirituality

MORE THAN YOU KNOW
ARIEON BURNS © 2016

My resentment for this establishment:
More than you know.
My animosity for their fake generosity:
I'm going to get my revenge on those who binge and purge distorted lies.

The admiration that I feel for that innocent creation:
More than you know.
He walks at a steadfast pace,
Racing through the lies and denouncements made about him.
He, too, feels how I do - deep inside.

We are similar in many ways;
Aphotic and robotic,
Wishing to break free from these bindings weaved from the white trash lies
of the world.
The river of deceit runs thick…
Flows rapidly.

Poetic Pearls & Gems With Purpose

I try and tread up river to safety,
Trying to break free from those who
carelessly talk with
free will and sureness.
That same pure creation is the one who
saved me from drowning;
Drowning in the lies of
what make up the world.

He sheltered me from the repulsive
people who are ugly on the inside;
Sacrificed Himself and left me begging
for Him to stay -
Alive and well…physically;
Alone and cast down…mentally.

All that remains is the
recollection of His voice,
Taped and played on repeat for the
enjoyment of not only me,
But for the people who pushed Him to
the breaking point;
The people who falsify His life and don't
glorify who He saved or
what He had made…
Which is more than you know.

Purpose Gem: Salvation & Spirituality

JESUS, MY FRIEND JESUS
MARLOWE R. SCOTT © 1995

What a friend we have in Jesus;
He all our sins and grief will bear.
Our friend, Jesus, came and left
Someone special
When He ascended to
His Father in the air!

The Comforter, the Holy Spirit,
Surrounds each of us every day
and everywhere;
Because our Beloved Counselor and
Friend, Jesus,
Left the Holy Spirit here - when He joined
His Father in the air!

But wait - Do you really know
my friend, Jesus?
Does He all your burdens bear?
Are you really ready to
meet and greet Him
When He descends again -
coming down through the air?

Poetic Pearls & Gems With Purpose

If not, then I invite you today
to receive Him
And enjoy the friendly,
bountiful love I share
With our Lord and Savior, Jesus Christ,
Who reigns in Heaven with God - up
there in the air!

Come quickly!
Praise and celebrate with me!
A Friend who loves unconditionally,
without compare;
His name is Emanuel - Wonderful Jesus,
be ye ready to meet Him
When He comes again from Glory -
shouting through the air!

Purpose Gem: Salvation & Spirituality

HIGHER SPIRITUAL HEIGHTS

MARLOWE R. SCOTT © 2013

The man of God came
preaching and teaching
About Jesus, the Savior and True Vine;
It is the message of being connected
To the Messiah, who came to save all mankind!

The congregation was
excited by the Word
And felt the Holy Spirit's fire;
God used the preacher as a messenger
To edify and lift Jesus higher!

The preacher's sermon
about the Day of Pentecost
Gave thirsty souls high
spiritual blessings and insight;
The congregation rejoiced
and praised God
For the valuable lesson on
growing in this spiritual fight!

Poetic Pearls & Gems With Purpose

As the man of God continues to lead,
Everything - yes, everything -
will be alright;
For thirsting souls to grow and be blessed
Until reaching God's promised
Heavenly Heights!

Purpose Gem: Salvation & Spirituality

GROWING IN FAITH
MARLOWE R. SCOTT © 2015

Our Spiritual Gift of Faith,
like the small mustard seed,
Is planted by God and must grow
Into a deep-rooted belief
that our Father nurtures
As the sun, winds, and
storms of life come and go.

While our fruitful day
may not readily come,
God continues the sunshine and rains
And counts each budding
leaf one by one.

You see: He knows the end before we do
Because all of His promises
are definitely true; and,
We must have faith to see the growing-
period through.

Poetic Pearls & Gems With Purpose

When we begin to mature and bear the fruit as we should,
We will see the positive outcome of those times we waited
And realize that our God surely has been more than good!

PURPOSE GEM:

SPECIAL ADDITIONS

Poetic Pearls & Gems With Purpose

SAVE THE CHILDREN, STOP THE VIOLENCE, KEEP THE PEACE

LOYCE BULLOCK © 2016

Throughout this world, day after day, our constant cry of the heart is *"Save the Children, Stop the Violence, Keep the Peace"*. This has been echoed so long that it is possible we have forgotten what it is we are crying about. It is relatively easy to believe that we no longer know, because the sound continues as a broken faucet: DRIP, DRIP, DRIP………

No one seems to know what the solution is, though we are making this a lifetime chore. Some of us seem to think that this is a career; sort of like finding a cure for cancer. We are putting in the hours, yet children are still dying………

Purpose Gem: Special Additions

Someone's time is being wasted because the tools needed to *Save the Children, Stop the Violence, and Keep the Peace* were discarded and thrown into the sea of forgetfulness many years ago at the hands of the Supreme Court..........

Without the proper tools, nothing can be changed; and if nothing changes, the crying will continue.

Is it really the goal of the people of this world to *Save the Children, Stop the Violence, and Keep the Peace*? Or is this goal merely an intent voiced to give us hope and something to believe in???????

If the minds of the people are occupied and everyone is feeling needed, then they won't ask for the things that will infringe upon the efforts of those in authority. Is it the old "Keep Them Occupied, Keep Them Happy" scenario???????

We must move forward, for today the solution is nigh. First, we must retrieve the tools that are needed to successfully implement the task of *Saving the Children, Stopping the Violence, and Keeping the Peace*. We are digging down deep. We see the tools; they are in our hands. But wait: Our goal can never be accomplished because we are not allowed to bring these tools back to life. We have been forbidden by law:

NO JESUS IN OUR PUBLIC SCHOOLS

So, long after we are dead, we can still hear the crying..........

**SAVE THE CHILDREN,
STOP THE VIOLENCE,
KEEP THE PEACE.**

Purpose Gem: Special Additions

THE DEVIL GOES TO CHURCH

BESSIE BRENT WINSTON © 1947
"ALABASTER BOXES"

The devil went to church one day,
And as he strolled along
He planned how he could execute
Some deeds of sin and wrong.

He did not stop down near the door,
As most outsiders would,
But went as close as he could get
To where the preacher stood.

He heard him read in earnest tones
Words from the Holy Book;
The devil turned and hurled at him
An ugly, angry look.

He heard him tell with gentle voice
The curse of sin and pain,
And strive to bring the straying sheep
Back to the fold again.

Poetic Pearls & Gems With Purpose

He heard him tell in wisdom's words
  Salvation's wondrous plan.
 The devil frowned and bit his lip
  And said, "I hate that man.

"I've done my best by day and night
  To lead his flock astray;
 He'll undo everything I've done,
  If he goes on this way."

So down the aisle he made his way
  To see what he could do
 Along the line of starting things
  And making trouble brew.

He saw two girls down near the door,
  With faces sweet and fair,
 With heads bowed low, as if they were
  In earnest, thoughtful prayer.

Straight to those girls the devil went
  And said, "Look at that hat
 That Sister Molly Gray has on,
  And Easter day at that!"

Purpose Gem: Special Additions

Then up from thoughts
of prayer and praise
Two pair of roguish eyes
Went straight to Sister Molly's hat
In mischievous surprise.

And then they bowed their heads again
And laughed and giggled till
The deacon had to go to them
And ask them to be still.

And then the devil took a seat
By Sister Mary Wood;
He knew she'd much prefer to hear
The bad instead of good.

He whispered something in her ear,
And then she turned her head
And whispered to the deacon's wife;
I don't know what she said.

But instantly the deacon's wife
Replied, "O dear, O dear,
If that is true, then I'll not pay
Another penny here."

Poetic Pearls & Gems With Purpose

The devil grinned and went his way,
His joy too deep to tell,
And as he went he murmured low,
"That worked out pretty well!"

And then he went to Brother Green -
He'd seen him yawn and gap.
He said, "Just lean your head on me,
And take a little nap."

He gently rocked him to and fro
Down dreamland's pathway steep
And sang him impish lullabies
Till he was fast asleep.

He saw a small boy passing by,
On some dire mischief bent;
Then down the aisle
and through the door
A wireless was sent.

It read like this: "Peep in the door
At good old Silas Blair;
He'll kneel in just a little while
To make a silly prayer.

Purpose Gem: Special Additions

"Just keep an eye, and when he does,
You throw a stone and run.
It won't be wrong, for every boy
Must have a little fun."

And so it happened that a stone
Came whizzing through the air
And made poor Brother Silas jump
And yell out in despair.

An 'Amen' brother, staunch and true,
Whose name was Aaron Kent,
Had in his worn-out pocketbook
A dollar and a cent.

He hadn't been to church for months,
And so had planned to spare
That dollar bill to sort of pay
For times he wasn't there.

The devil sat down by his side
And whispered in his ear,
"You're just as crazy as a bat
To pay that dollar here.

Poetic Pearls & Gems With Purpose

"The church clerk and the treasurer, too,
    Are crooked as can be.
They always take their spending change
    From out of the treasury.

"Where do you think the treasurer's wife
    Gets all her fancy clothes?
She never does a lick of work,
    But dresses up and goes.

"That clerk has got a brand new car,
    All shiny, black, and sleek;
Folks don't go in for cars like that
    On twenty-five per week.

So take your dollar bill straight home
    And put your penny in;
To help those crooked folks along
    Would really be a sin."

So when the plate was passed around,
    Good Brother Aaron Kent
Kept back the nice new dollar bill
    And gave the church the cent.

Purpose Gem: Special Additions

The devil smacked him on the back
And said, "That's fine, old dear,
And don't you ever, ever give
More than a penny here."

A little girl named Rosabelle
Who came from Tennessee,
Was chairman of a junior club
They called The Busy Bee.

The club had labored faithfully
Through each hot Summer day,
Till twenty-four bright bills
In their small treasury lay.

The devil said to Rosabelle,
"That hat at Kimberly's
Has been reduced to four-nineteen;
It's pretty as can be.

"Why don't you go and get that hat
Before Jane Spencer does?
She always thinks she looks so nice;
Don't hesitate, because…

Poetic Pearls & Gems With Purpose

"Part of that money's yours by rights;
You worked just like a mule;
To give the church the whole of it,
You'd be a little fool."

And so on next church meeting day,
The lovely Rosabelle
Was dressed up in a brand new hat,
And purse and gloves as well.

He found his way up in the choir,
Where only peace belongs,
And sitting down cross-legged, went
To meddling with the song.

He whispered in a sister's ear,
"This isn't fair a bit;
Unless they sang the hymns I liked,
If I were you, I'd quit."

And then an ugly selfish look
Came in that sister's eyes,
And made the organist look up
In sad and grave surprise.

Purpose Gem: Special Additions

He made the tenors laugh and talk
Till there was not a trace
Of order in the choir stand;
It bordered on disgrace.

He then walked up and down the aisle
And looked at everyone,
To see if there was anything
That he had left undone.

He really wasn't satisfied;
He could have spent the day
Rejoicing in his devilment
And leading folks astray.

The sermon being over now,
The devil got his hat
And said, "I wish I'd had more time,
But 'twasn't bad at that."

And when he snuggled down to sleep,
His imps all heard him say,
"I'm tired as a man can be,
But what a happy day!"

THE END

Poetic Pearls & Gems With Purpose

CONCLUSION

Poetry is truly amazing. The freedom of thought is a gift from God - as proven evident in the works submitted here.

You, Dear Reader, are not told how to feel as you read each poem. Rather, the intent is for you to interpret the meanings and how they connect with your spirit-man / spirit-woman. Each author brings forth an emotion felt "in the moment" from their specific source of inspiration: love, peace, joy, pain, heartache, and yes, even laughter.

As Compiler of this awesome work, it is my sincere prayer that you have been inspired, encouraged, healed, and/or uplifted in some way.

Poetic Pearls & Gems With Purpose

I leave you with the following passage of Scripture and pray you stand fast in the Lord today and always:

"Finally, brethren, whatever things are true, whatever things are noble, whatever things are just, whatever things are pure, whatever things are lovely, whatever things are of good report, if there is any virtue and if there is anything praiseworthy - meditate [think] on these things."

Philippians 4:8 (NKJV)

~ Angela R. Edwards ~

PURPOSE GEM:

PEN YOUR POEM

Use the following section to free-write a poem. What are *YOU* feeling in **THIS** exact moment?

Poetic Pearls & Gems With Purpose

Purpose Gem: Pen Your Poem

Poetic Pearls & Gems With Purpose

Purpose Gem: Pen Your Poem

Poetic Pearls & Gems With Purpose

Purpose Gem: Pen Your Poem

Poetic Pearls & Gems With Purpose

APPENDIX

Winston, B.B. (1947). *Alabaster boxes* (1st ed.). Takoma Park, WA, D.C.: Review and Herald Publishing Association.

ABOUT THE COMPILER

Angela R. Edwards is the CEO of Pearly Gates Publishing LLC (PGP), an International Christian Book Publisher based out of Houston, Texas (USA). The vision of PGP sprang to life in early January 2015 after God gave Angela the mission to bring to the world authors whose desires encompass **keeping** their God-given inspiration in their literary works. Founded in February 2015, the business has continued to blossom into a sought-after publishing house for both current and up-and-coming Christian authors worldwide. At the time of this writing, PGP's youngest authors are ages eight and 10, and the oldest is 72, with authors from the United States, Uganda Africa, and Clonmel County, Tipperary, Ireland.

Poetic Pearls & Gems With Purpose

Pearly Gates Publishing LLC is a low-cost publishing option for individuals seeking to spread their messages of empowerment, inspiration, and education. Since its inception, PGP has produced numerous Amazon Best Sellers - with three making the coveted number one spot. A variety of topics from PGP's authors include (but are not limited to):

- ➢ Faith
- ➢ Bullying
- ➢ Post-Traumatic Stress Disorder
- ➢ Autism
- ➢ Domestic Violence
- ➢ Poetry
- ➢ Salvation
- ➢ And SO much more!

Contact Angela TODAY! Let's work together to "get **THAT** book out of *YOU!*"

Poetic Pearls & Gems With Purpose

CONNECT WITH PEARLY GATES PUBLISHING LLC

Web:
www.PearlyGatesPublishing.com

Facebook:
www.facebook.com/PearlyGatesPublishing

Instagram:
www.instagram.com/PGPublishing

YouTube:
www.youtube.com/PearlyGatesPublishing

Twitter:
www.twitter.com/PearlyPublish

Email:
BestSeller@PearlyGatesPublishing.com

PHONE: (832) 230-9443

Mail: P.O. Box 62287, Houston, TX 77205

www.ingramcontent.com/pod-product-compliance
Lightning Source LLC
Chambersburg PA
CBHW071527080526
44588CB00011B/1581